REMEMBERING
A Love

A Widow's Inside Journey

REMEMBERING A Love

A Widow's Inside Journey

MARGARET PALCZYNSKI DUNBAR

Pentland Press, Inc.
www.pentlandpressusa.com

PUBLISHED BY PENTLAND PRESS, INC.
5122 Bur Oak Circle, Raleigh, North Carolina 27612
United States of America
919-782-0281

ISBN 1-57197-233-1
Library of Congress Control Number: 00-132884

Printed in the United States of America

In memory of

RAYMOND

who forever dances in my heart,

and for

JANE

who also knows widowhood.

Table of Contents

Preface

To this day, I can vividly recall that I was taking a math exam when the P.A. announcement interrupted my focused concentration. President John F. Kennedy had been shot in Dallas.

Throughout the next days of that bleak November, I was struck by Jackie Kennedy's demeanor. Some called it stoic; others called it strong. Even at seventeen, I sensed that her courage was possible because of some inner space.

I didn't know then how widowhood would strike my family—never making the front page, but deeply turning the tide of lives. My sister, Jane, became a widow at the age of twenty-six. She had a fifteen-month-old daughter and was three months pregnant. I became a widow at the age of forty and had a six-year-old daughter.

During the immediate days following my husband's death, I found solace in writing. In the days, weeks, months, and years that followed, I filled journals, grieving at ever deeper levels.

This is an account of my own personal inside journey. What I have written is rooted in my living one day at a time. It is the fruit of my efforts to give voice to the inner experience of grief. Words shaped the silence of my inner agony while the outer demands necessitated that I keep going.

Day by day I wrote what filled me even as I longed to wordlessly express my soul in the embrace of a lover. At times the words shaped the silence of my lived inner agony. At other times they were simply a release so that I could re-gather courage to move through the pain. At times writing offered healing. Occasionally, writing led me to a creative breakthrough enabling me to tap new energy reserves.

When we experience a loss, we are invited to feel, grieve, and enter into the pain so that we can move through it and let go. What is that like day by day? I seem to have to tackle the web of grief one small thread at a time. Writing helped me to break down what I was experiencing, so that I allowed myself to feel the loss over and over in a variety of little ways and slowly let go.

"The death of a spouse—one of the most emotionally disruptive events of a person's life—is experienced by more than

80,000 people every year." (Shuchter 1986). When that death is sudden, the disruption is massively disorientating, with no time to say good-bye while the beloved is still living. When dying takes a slower course, death can come as a relief to the beloved's suffering, but the loss is no less disorienting.

Although each person's story is unique, what is most personal is often most universal. I have tried to faithfully tell the story of my inside journey, selecting journal entries as they were actually written in the moments after my husband's death. It is my hope that what I have come to know about myself and express about my journey can touch others. In remembering a love:

—I join with the widowed, in their journey, perhaps expressing some unspoken grief.

—I invite the partnered to reappreciate the other with whom they are privileged to struggle and rejoice.

—I reach out to all feeling people who know the power of love that is stronger than death.

Acknowledgments

I extend my heartfelt gratitude to:

. . . the Spirit within me, inviting, inspiring and urging me to write.

. . . my daughter, Laura Hope Dunbar, the gift of a remembered love, for her courage to feel her feelings, grieve her loss, and recreate her life with hope.

. . . my mother-in-law and father-in-law, Genevieve and the late Raymond T. Dunbar, Sr., who gave my husband, Raymond, life and suffered the loss of their son.

. . . my parents, Michael and Bernice Palczynski, who have loved together for fifty-seven years and from whom I learned love.

. . . my sister, Jane Marie Consiglio, who inspired me with her courage when her husband Jack died at the young age of twenty-four.

. . . my friends, Mary Eckert and Kevin Kerbawy, who knew Raymond, read and blessed the manuscript in its early stages.

. . . my colleague, Margaret Haggerty, who read the manuscript and invited me to add an epilogue.

. . . my colleague, Victoria Duley, for producing the manuscript from my penned pages.

. . . my book's "midwives," the staff of Pentland Press, for trusting and supporting my desire to voice the often unspoken feelings and emotions connected with grief. They have helped me to give birth to *Remembering a Love*.

And finally, I am profoundly grateful for the ways in which we are all connected through the remembered loves of our lifetimes.

My Inside Journey

The feather flutters to my heart

falling on silent tears

You dance there forever

though I no longer can touch you . . .

And as you dance

in

my

heart

I hear the song of my soul

leading me home

inviting me to do with integrity

what I love along the way.

MPD
8/14/93
at Commonweal
Bolinas, California

Part One: DEATH

(My Father looked at a bird lying on its side against the curb near our house.)

"Is it dead, Papa?" I was six and could not bring myself to look at it.

"Yes." I heard him say in a sad and distant way.

"Why did it die?"

"Everything that lives must die."

"Everything?"

"Yes."

"You too Papa? And Mama?"

"Yes."

"And me?"

"Yes," he said. Then he added in Yiddish, "But may it be only after you live a long and good life, my Asher."

I could not grasp it. I forced myself to look at the bird. Everything alive would one day be as still as that bird.

"Why?" I asked.

"That's the way the ribbono Shel Olom made His world, Asher."

"Why?"

"So life would be precious, Asher. Something that is yours forever is never precious."

—Chaim Potok

We can fight our dying, but death itself is inescapable. Whether one suffers a long illness or a sudden death, the still moment of finally dying is irreversible. This cutting off, when one passes out of temporal time and space, marks a finality.

Like a tree cut through at the base, death brings a final felling. The tree may have reached maturity and is to be used for fine lumber. Or perhaps it is diseased and cannot be treated. It may be a young tree being cleared to make space and light and water available to surrounding trees. Whatever the circumstances of its lumbering, there is still the moment of the tree's final fall. A fresh cut aroma lingers in the days after its cutting. The scent triggers a remembering of the freshness. Yet never again will the tree bear new leaves.

On Thursday, March 12, 1987, my husband died at 4:25 P.M. He was pronounced dead at 5:15 P.M. He was laid to rest beneath a majestic fir tree on March 16. Part One describes the journey of those four days. His death was announced; his life was remembered and celebrated.

Somehow I moved through those days calling on every resource within my being and body. Familiar rituals, neighborly generosity, family bonds, and friends' support helped carry me through. Those days were like time out of time. I did not yet experience the grief of missing my husband in ordinary time. That was yet to be.

For four days, I, and those who knew and loved him, confronted his death. Only in the months ahead would its finality truly register.

Giving Voice to Loss

March 12, 1987
4:25 P.M.

I watch my beloved husband, who just hours earlier was at his potent best, being lifted into the ambulance. The siren sounds and they rush him to the hospital. A police officer offers to drive me to the hospital. In these moments, as we drive down familiar streets, with neighbors standing in silent helpless witness, I am silent. I know Raymond has died even as I hope and pray for a second chance. I know that I am loved and will be strengthened. I am not numb. I am feeling at my depths.

5:05 P.M.

I go to the pay phone and contact Raymond's parents.

5:15 P.M.

A nurse sits with me, holds my hand, and says, "Margaret, they're doing everything they can. It doesn't look good."

"I know," I say. And I already do.

This is the knowing of aloneness, a knowing beyond which I've ever known, a knowing like a sword piercing my heart, a knowing that will change me forever. I am shaken to the core of my being.

5:20 P.M. The doctor comes out. I stand up, almost as if I am to receive a sentence. He tells me that Raymond is gone. There was nothing they could do. (It was a massive heart attack.)

He turns and leaves. I sob and weep. My knowing is public.

I ask to see my husband and walk into the emergency room beyond the curtains. There lies my beloved. I touch his face and kiss his eyes and ears and mouth. I move my hands down his chest and arms and lay my head on his now-still heart. My tears wash him as I hear only the stillness. The heartbeat, to which I could listen for hours, especially loving to rest my head on his chest after we made love, is now silent. I kiss his penis and run my hands down his legs and his big, wide feet. I re-cover him and hold him as best as my arms can enwrap his body.

I walk out and friends compassionately embrace me, and we cry together. Immediately there are details and papers to sign.

It is not until 2:00 A.M. that I am finally alone. I have made phone calls, received family and friends, held my six-year-old daughter to sleep, and then come into the family room alone. Absorbing the silence, I cry out my inconsolable grief: "Why?! Why?! Why?!" I still can't take it in . . .

Friday, March 13; Saturday, March 14, 1987

The days proceed in timeless space as people come to pay tribute. And on the casket, a single red rose with my note:

> *Dearest Raymond,*
> > *How I celebrate your peace!*
> > *How I miss you!*
> > > *My enduring love,*
> > > *Margaret*

Sunday, March 16, 1987

I awake early and again seek alone, introverted time. I need this, more than food these days to sustain my spirit. I cry and cry, so wanting to communicate with Raymond. And so I write him a letter. The writing is for me; yet speaking it will be for him.

> *My dearest Raymond,*
> *How I miss you! So many times already, I have thought/felt for a brief moment, "I'll tell Raymond that or run that by Raymond." Only to realize that I will never again hear your voice, never touch you, never experience the tenderness of your affirmation, the gentleness of your love, the gruffness of our discussions. I am so much the woman I am and know so much of the wholeness I know in my soul this day because of our love and commitment. I ache that you struggled so to tell me that you loved me. But you gave me a great gift on the day of your death during your presentation to the counselors, about family systems, when you publicly proclaimed your love and*

commitment. That would be your way to be intimate—as extroverted as could be. And I accepted you, received your love, and felt so close to you that morning.

How I longed to grow old with you; and yet somehow, in my own limited, intuitive way, I knew that our time together was to be only a small part of our lives. I knew and loved you for a decade of my life; my thirties coming into forty were blessed by the interaction which fosters intimacy. And my love is enduring, Raymond, for as I came to accept you and honor you in your separateness, I could choose more each day to love you. And my desire for you, as I stripped away all my expectations, was your peace. In some small way, perhaps my love freed you to find what you sought with your whole being. And somehow that couldn't be on this side. You are free now, Raymond, free from responsibility, free to know the truth and experience the light in fullness. You are free to make music, and I want to keep hearing your songs. So does Laura.

You see the face of god/goddess for which I so long. Our faith unites us in a way it never has. And our friends sustain me and Laura in a way they never have. I feel like my whole life has prepared me to live these days and what they will ask. My journey must continue. You may know my path more clearly than I.

And our dear Laura, Raymond. I am so angry that she will not know you as she passes through her milestones. I hear from everyone how she was your pride and joy, how you spoke of her. She loves you so and wants you back. I'll be coming to the cemetery often to talk with you about her. I can only give her that part of you that I have taken into myself. You must watch out for your daughter from up there. See to it that she stays safe and can grow because she knows that she is loved and lovable. I so want Laura to be a child through all this—she has to grow up fast enough. How I ache as the tears flow. How silent and alone is my solitude this morning knowing you are not present.

Freed and at peace, channel strength my way; not the strength that is unfeeling and endures but the strength that is centered and flows from the core of my pain and hurt and love. The celebrations today and tomorrow are our gifts to our families and friends and community. I can almost hear you accompanying on the guitar.

I sense people will talk about this as they do about our wedding, Raymond. And in that way, together, we have touched lives because of our love and commitment. My image of marriage always held that sense of what would be because of two coming together and creating something unable to be born from either alone. I want people to know this without a doubt, and so I'm going to have to be extroverted and immediate and present in inviting them to new life. But I'm scared, too. Can I face the people and feel and still be centered enough to communicate? I want to do this for you, for me, for those who love us. So please channel centered strength my way.

I'm going to say all this to you tomorrow because that's what you'd like. I write it now to honor that part of me that needs nurturing. So get ready, Raymond, because we're going to go at it one more time while your body is still visible to me.

Monday, March 16, 1987

My beloved is buried and laid to rest.

I awaken early, and in the western sky against the blue, cloudless sky is a full moon. It is Raymond's kind of morning—with a crisp nip in the air. I want to be with Raymond and go over to church where he already lies. As the day dawns, the sun filters through the colored glass windows, warming my shoulders and the head of the casket.

I touch Raymond's head, hair, ears, cold nose. I kiss his eyelids, as I did every night before we went to sleep, and then his cold lips. I massage his chest and arms and feel his hands.

I hold my hand on his heart for the longest time, feeling the stone-coldness. And then I finger his beard, delighting in the fact that in hair there is not a change as quickly. I rub my fingers through it, tickle him, scratch it, weeping, letting my tears flow all over his suit and shirt and face, telling him how much I love him. And I pound his chest—Why didn't you let me love you?!? I so wanted to be there for you and grow old with you . . .

And then, thinking back to our wedding day, I recalled putting the wedding ring on his finger. Now holding his hand, I tenderly take the ring off his cold frozen finger, twisting it over his knuckle, knowing that a chapter in the journey of my life ends today, even though the book continues to be written. But I told Raymond that he knew how much I enjoyed rereading good books, so this chapter was going to be reread a lot.

As I left the church, the sun was shining through the southeast windows toward the casket with light filtered beams. There was a song in my heart and a deep, deep sense of peace that something holy was about to take place.

Part Two: DARKNESS

"Whom will you cry to, heart?

More and more lonely,

your path struggles on . . ."

—Rainer Maria Rilke, "Lament."

The death of one with whom we have shared dailyness and ordinariness plunges us into grief and mourning and darkness. Something precious and unfolding is now cut off.

After a giant tree falls, the remaining stump is still a reminder of the tree's life and presence. Eventually that too is removed, and a deep hole, which held the roots and all that nourished the tree's life, now forms. The chasm becomes deeper as the earth shifts and settles. No amount of immediately filling up the hole can obliterate the missing of the tree. It is as if the earth remembers.

The death of my husband was very disorientating, plunging me into a deep, internal darkness. The familiar presence, the daily routines, the comfortable rituals were suddenly missing. No amount of "filling up the hole" dissipates the darkness; it only obliterates it for a time. Rather, one has to enter the darkness and experience the void. Entering into these feelings as fully as one can is the crucible wherein the healing and recovery occur—within the vessel of one's broken being.

Part Two describes the darkness of the first year after my husband's death. Although death occurs in a moment, comprehending the loss it brings takes time. Describing the agony in words named the innumerable losses which I had to experience.

It takes courage not to fill up the hole too quickly. It takes courage to experience the chasm and slowly acknowledge the loss. Although his death occurred in a moment in time, I had to learn to say good-bye again and again. It took so much energy to go forward without R.— groping through the darkness to find the light, to find an opening in the grief.

Giving Voice to Grief

Tuesday, March 17, 1987

Just when I feel I could hurt no more, the hurt is deeper than ever and seems to be unbearable . . .

Sunday, March 22, 1987

My faith continues to sustain me, and on that level I know a deep peace for and with R. Humanly, I ache so, feeling this evening so robbed of a history with R., of growing old together. I may grow old with friends but shall not have that dailyness of intimacy and growth with another. I hurt . . . I ache . . . I am so scared . . .

Monday, March 23, 1987

I sob myself to sleep last night. The physical fatigue begins to take its toll . . . I miss R.'s touch and presence. I ache in missing R., sharing decisions, celebrating spring on a beautiful morning, delighting in Laura.

Monday, March 30, 1987

I turn toward R.'s side of the bed, missing his presence and feeling the pain of our incompleteness.

Friday, April 3, 1987

My love endures as I cry such tears of grief and sadness. I am sad and grieve the passion we never expressed. I grieve the history we will no longer make together. I miss you, my spouse, my lover, my friend.

No one, not my closest friends, can know or understand the deep paradox of what I am feeling and aching.

Saturday, April 4, 1987

I walk in the early morning wind, singing your songs. I know an energy and feel loss so deeply.

Sunday, April 5, 1987

Tomorrow I will resume more regular routines. I ask for strength and staying power, for centeredness and softness . . .

Friday, April 10, 1987

Today would have been your thirty-ninth birthday. Laura wanted to have a party. So we went to McDonald's for breakfast and then to the cemetery. We sang two of your songs and left a balloon at your grave.

Later as I read the mail, I break into such sounds of sobbing . . . I am gripped with convulsive grieving. My whole body shakes with tremors. I sob and sob from my soul. There is no comfort at all . . .

Sunday, April 12, 1987

One month anniversary of your death.

I let myself feel as my whole body weeps.

Paradoxically, I give thanks for the aloneness which allows me to go down and grieve at new levels so as to continue to release R.

Good Friday, April 17, 1987

I am gripped by the words "It is finished!" I go to the cemetery and weep and sob as I speak the words, "It is finished!" You have handed over your spirit, dearest Raymond. How I grieve! I love you, Raymond. I miss you!

I re-live the scenes of your death as your spirit left you, as you handed yourself over. I recall the weight of your head as we turned you over to do CPR. And then your still, silent body in the hospital emergency room. I knew in our home that you had died, but held onto some hope until the doctor "pronounced" you dead, until I heard the words, "It is finished!"

Saturday, April 18, 1987

Today I dream that R. came back, that he was alive and among us again.

I awake, questioning if R. was back; turned to my left and looked in bed. I have to re-learn that he is dead.

Thursday, April 23, 1987

Today I take a mental health day. I feel so vulnerable, so weary. The newness of each day presents ways that R. keeps dying in me every hour, every moment. I feel deep in my soul this invitation to let go, but only after and if I have deeply felt and grieved. I know loss at deeper and deeper levels.

I am coming to slowly know and understand that the loss I know is much more inclusive than R.'s death alone. His death, his absence, is like a pebble in a deep pool which ripples out in ever-widening circles, as I feel loss:

—as a spouse; I am not married any longer.

—as a parent; I am a single parent now.

—as a family; we are a family of two instead of three.

—of companionship; I can't process my thinking and feeling with R.

—of presence, especially in the joy of R.'s music.

—of how I relate to other adults, now as a widow.

—of the boundary and commitment of marriage which freed me to relate to other men easily; now will my affection be read differently?

In letting you go, I am closer to you than ever. But ever so fleetingly.

I remember your dying, as you spoke, "I'm so afraid." I often sensed your deep fears. What a great gift you gave yourself and me when you acknowledged your fear. Did you know at that moment that everything was slipping from you?

Gently, carefully, patiently, I am learning forms of new love with you. When I touch my wedding ring, I sense such a deep connectedness to you. We are stripped of masks, pretenses, fears. We stand before each other naked and healed.

For you, healing meant wholeness in a new form, a new way.

For me, healing means feeling my pain and claiming my own power. I can do this because I am a woman who has been loved, is loved, and who chooses to love. And so the question is no longer, "How am I going to interact with you?" but, "How am I going to remember you?" For as I remember, I honor what was good and bold and beautiful about you!

Loving tears flow from the depths of my heart and soul now. Sometimes I feel like I'm going to break, but really I am just being stretched to feel more and more deeply.

Friday, April 24, 1987

I've hugged a lot but it has been so long since someone actually held me.

Saturday, April 25, 1987

We receive a few more scattered items from your office—I laugh and cry. How I miss your creative spirit, your uniqueness. How I miss loving you daily!

Sunday, May 3, 1987

Today my eyes burn from the salt of my tears as I cry out my raw, deep grief.

Saturday, May 9, 1987

Though weakened and weary, I am coming to know my strength, a strength tendered by allowing pain to flow through me, by knowing suffering, a struggle inviting simplicity and grounding me.

Tuesday, May 12, 1987

I pack up and give away the remainder of R.'s clothes. His washed shirts hang in a row on hangers—the warm brown one, the new mauve one I got him for Christmas. And after a final washing of his clothes, I no longer smell his cologne. I ache to touch him, to smell him, to reach out in tenderness, to embrace as husband and wife, to make love as spouses. I just let myself feel the ache.

Thursday, May 14, 1987

I miss who R. was, not what I wanted him to become. I miss my husband—the man to whom I committed a lifetime of loving. That was permanent; his death is permanent.

Sunday, May 17, 1987

A new week, a new day . . .
This morning I celebrate:
—morning
—the sun
—newly potted plants
—magnificence of my peace lily
—memory
—the moment inviting healing and hope
—hope
—being loved
—humanness
—weakness

Wednesday, May 20, 1987

Morning silence is so silent; I let it envelop me.

Thursday, May 21, 1987

Tonight I am struck by how much I really wanted to be and chose to be married. How I miss being married . . . How I miss being spouse . . .

Marriage is the opportunity to offer the gift of the total person to another . . .

Saturday, May 23, 1987

Today I wonder—with whom I will grow old?!?

Sunday, May 24, 1987

Damn it, why did you have to up and die, R.?

How I wanted to grow old with you and delight in the unfolding of your gifts and talents. The absence of your created music haunts me. I miss you! I feel so raw today.

Monday, May 25, 1987—Memorial Day

We go to the cemetery and walk. It is comforting to bond with others who grieve the loss of loved ones. And yet I am struck that in the loss are the bonds. I still love R.; I know he loves me; we will be together some day—transformed in our love.

Tuesday, June 2, 1987

I invested so much energy in hoping, loving, standing by R. I even have to let go of this positive investment. There is no hope with R. anymore. I have to pull up anchor, so as to be able to re-anchor my hope . . .

Wednesday, June 3, 1987

Today I am sad. Making our home mine is necessary but difficult and requires such a wrenching . . .

Wednesday, June 10, 1987

I receive some photos and spontaneously want to show them to R. I feel a sadness initially; then I go inside and touch him there.

Friday, June 12, 1987

Death is really NOT a good-bye, but you have to say good-bye. You have to let go of the outer to have the peace within you to experience presence and communion in a new way. Another of life's paradoxes.

Monday, June 15, 1987

I am alone as breadwinner/wage earner.

I am alone in parenting.

I ache, I ACHE; I ACHE and ACHE!

I want to be held and comforted and nourished lovingly. I want to hear that it will be OK, when all I feel is overwhelmed. I sob and ACHE. I am so raw; new wounds are continually re-opened and can hardly heal before I feel pain and loss at new levels. Not to feel this is death, but to feel takes so much . . . I feel weak as I let go.

I am not depressed, but I am sad.

I hurt.

I ache.

I am not despairing, but I feel the cavernous space left as I let go of hopes:

—hopes for our marriage

—hopes for R.'s growth and new life

—hopes of growing old together

—hopes of learning from each other's oppositeness

I am not discouraged; I garner courage each day but not without tremendous cost to my energy reserves.

That's what I need to replenish through beauty, nature, time with friends. Nature asks only to be respected; it is nondemanding as I bask in its beauty.

I pause. I've nourished myself with some cherries and enjoy their sweet round coolness. It feels good to be taking delight anew.

I give great thanks for the courage to be with myself tonight.

Sunday, June 21, 1987

It is Father's Day, my daughter's sixth but the first without her father.

I take an afternoon nap and dream:

> *I'm in a large, airy, white house. Lots of relatives from afar have been staying there. It is Sunday afternoon; they, Laura, and I all take naps. Upon awakening, they finish packing and leave (as if they've been there for R.'s funeral.) My daughter is still napping.*
>
> *I walk into a light, airy windowed porch area. R. appears. I embrace him with my left arm, as we both look forward. I tell him I miss him. I begin crying; he cries; we weep together. Through the tears, he looks at me with an "I'm sorry" in his eyes. He holds me close as we cry, leaning on my shoulder, almost crying into me, saying, "I'm so sorry, Meig."*

This affirms and invites new levels of forgiveness.

Monday, June 22, 1987

I miss Raymond deeply as I continue to let go of our hopes together. I even miss some of the struggle, which was one expression of our passion.

Saturday, June 27, 1987

I feel a deep acceptance of my "lot" in life, based on the lessons I'm learning as well as the gracefulness with which I am moving through all these burdensome tasks and decisions.

At the same time I know an exhaustion.

How will I address my neediness?

How will I nourish myself?

I function and yet feel so confused and almost tormented.

Sunday, June 28, 1987

Last night I moved to the middle of the bed and turned on my left side facing R.'s "side of the bed." A flood of memories fills me, passes in a flood. I am convulsed with such grieving, such sobbing. I cry out loud, hoping not to awaken Laura. I struggle with calling a friend, wanting to be held, if only in spirit, but choose to feel my aloneness, my personal agony, my deepening grief.

I cry out with such a desperate sound begging R. to live even as I know he has died. The permanence grips me anew.

Monday, June 29, 1987

The grave marker sketch is ready . . . I know seeing my beloved's name in that way will impact anew.

I am needy and need to be strengthened. I want to move through completing thank you notes, grieve anew, and close that chapter. It is time . . .

Wednesday, July 1, 1987

How can I physically express the anger/rage I carry inside? I consider martial arts.

Friday, July 3, 1987

I awake groggily with dreams of R., not knowing if he is spirit, ghost, resurrected. I'm afraid to take his pulse and "find out." I've cried and sobbed and wailed alone, but with limited voice. I feel such an utter sadness and grief that I am so afraid of my own voice, of my sounds. Am I afraid someone might yell at me?

Saturday, July 4, 1987

Today we gather to celebrate the holiday. I relate and play on the outside. I hurt and cry and feel such grief on the inside.

Sunday, July 5, 1987

I continue my journey into ineffable mystery by finally having the courage to go down into the basement into R.'s hobby space. I sit in his tall black chair and let myself feel the cost of dashed hopes. I clench and pound my fists, so angry that R. can't receive my love. I call out loud, "I'm not married!" but know how much I continue to love R. in a new way. I spontaneously remove my wedding ring from my left hand and replace it on my right hand.

Saturday, July 11, 1987

I know rage and anger as I recall ways in which R. didn't take care of himself. But what matters more is that he was here, that he lived and loved, that I responded fully, knowing anger as well as love, that we learned together that those two can coexist. Toward whom else have I not only felt but expressed such deep anger and deep love? I knew commitment with him. I am different forever because of it. I know inside!

I have been wearing my wedding ring on my right hand this past week. It feels right to see its absence on my left hand—I am not married—and to feel its newness on my right hand—a different way of loving R. I experience the awkwardness as well and feel more ready to let go. I recall the power of putting my ring on each morning after a shower, with a firm sense of recommitment. And often, in the midst of struggle, I would touch it, recalling "precious and unique," feeling its bumpy contours. I miss wearing it, but recognize its power as a symbol all the more in not wearing it! I feel a deep ache and a deep joy. I know loss at new depths but feel the stirrings of new life as well.

Sunday, July 12, 1987

Today is four months since R. died. As I listen to the sounds of my broken heart, I know such a stripping—removing masks and stopgap measures, peeling down to the core—to stand naked and alone.

Wednesday, July 15, 1987

As I am more and more willing to feel, to go through my void, to experience my aloneness, to acknowledge my wounds, there is a knowing space within me. That knowing gives strength and direction to the driving power of my love; it is such a force for new life, for myself and others.

Loving and being loved has made all the difference in my life.

Wednesday, July 22, 1987

How I miss loving you, R.

Friday, July 23, 1987

Today I gave away our king-sized bed.

I'm almost too tired to feel my grief or sadness.

Friday, July 31, 1987

We return from spending a few days camping. Nature's simplest images touch my soul and quietly heal.

How like life in all its unfolding is the dance of the waves on the beach—ever changing, its beauty in the present moment to be observed, taken in, enjoyed, only to be washed away and changed with the next wave.

How unlike nature I often am, wanting rather to cling. How she teaches me to be and delight in the now, ever faithfully present in beauty and power.

I walk the beach feeling so needy, feeling my utter aloneness. A little sandpiper appears on the newly washed shore sand. She seems so fragile, and yet even as I hold that thought, she takes off in strong flight over the incoming waves, almost saying to me, you can do it. Yes, you feel fragile, but you have a power.

A sandpiper appears . . .

. . .and I am not alone.

I come to know anew how much a part of everything I am, and how much everything is a part of me.

Saturday, August 1, 1987

I peacefully welcome sleep on my new bed and invite healing dreams.

Sunday, August 2, 1987

I feel the rhythms of my grieving.

I seek solitude to mourn my beloved R. while being sought out by people. And yet, somehow, because of what I have been willing to feel, I can invite healing in them.

Wednesday, August 12, 1987

Today is five months since R.'s death. The twelfth holds a significance it never had before.

I am moved to listen to a Leo Kottke album, "My Feet are Smiling." It's a way you are here, dearest. I feel your energy in the dissonance I hear. I know your soul and am connected to you, missing you so. And I thank you for gifting me with new music, for teaching me to hear with my heart and my body. I see you in your shiny black wedding shoes—your feet dancing and smiling, your fingers playing the strings of your guitar with such tenderness, agility, know-how, like you played the "chords" of my body. How I miss your touch! I miss the music you made with your hands, your soul, your whole being. You are here through Leo Kottke's gift. I love and embrace you, my beloved, as I weep from my depths.

The grave marker has been set in place at the cemetery. You are now honored and named at your burial site. Somehow now it's okay for me to go on anew and begin the school year without you. I am ready to re-enter and face the mystery of autumn, your favorite season, without you present here in your body.

Friday, August 21, 1987

I ache in missing you.

I miss being married.

I miss being committed to another. (In fact, by habit I still feel for my wedding ring on my finger each morning like I used to— recommitting myself to love and honor you this day.)

I miss the friction, the rubbing, the conflict that fostered growth and love.

I miss the dailyness.

I miss sharing the newness, awareness, and insights of this new school year beginning.

I miss loving you and unwinding with you and being a family.

And I think about truly what a Renaissance man you were:

—artist and scientist

—musician and administrator

—spiritual depth and insight

—appreciation for history and an eye to the future

And yet neglect of your body hindered these all flowering into a continuing wholeness.

Saturday, August 22, 1987

I sob from such a depth; how I miss loving you.

How I miss you! I fear the memory of your light and goodness will fade. I long and cry out to hear your voice one more time, to hear a song, to hear your guitar, to feel your touch, to scratch your beard, to kiss you. Oh, how I miss you, my love!

Loving you tapped my energy and creativity, my instincts and femininity; the memory of loving you taps a deep void.

Sunday, August 23, 1987

Sometimes I fear I will forget you, that my memories will dim. And so I hold on so tightly, perhaps when I most need to let go.

Monday, August 24, 1987

How I ache in wanting you back. After settling Laura to sleep and debriefing, I would have enjoyed lying with you, gently stroking your back or belly, each arousing the other to a playful rhythm, and then making love. Somehow in that creative act of gathering and uniting and loving, the dailyness epitomizes the sacredness which it is.

Today I met the woman hired for your job. This has been one of the most difficult milestones marking how life goes on. When I read in the newspaper, "filling position held by the late Raymond Dunbar," I weep.

Saturday, August 29, 1987

In a very real way, my woman/adult/child feels abandoned by R. I feel forsaken and deserted. I have had power taken away—the power that is released through the bond of marriage, through shared parenting, through the joys and sorrows and challenges and demands of family life.

I feel so close to breaking so often, calling on every inner resource to muster the courage to hold and feel and be touched by the pain, the ache, the emptiness.

I know my sadness and own it so as not to be immobilized by its grip.

Monday, August 31, 1987

I dream of you, asking you to help out with tasks.

I am exhausted.

Wednesday, September 2, 1987

Today would have been our ninth wedding anniversary.

I trust you hear the cry of my broken heart.

I entrust all I feel to your tenderness, my God.

I stop at the cemetery and release R. from carrying parts for me (play, creativity, craziness). I ask R. to release me from carrying parts for him. In these two simple statements of release, I know some space for new life!

Thursday, September 3, 1987

As I more deeply, vividly, frequently, and concretely remember R., I am being invited to let go of what could have been. I am being invited to reclaim the parts he carried (playfulness, creativity) and reclaim my power as me—not as living out R.'s script or completing what he began. R.'s "unfinished" life must be just that—unfinished. I carry him within me with a new lightness.

Friday, September 4, 1987

Today I finally completed the last of the thank-you notes. This has been a time-consuming but important ritual for me.

I feel empty, not in the sense of a void, but open and willing and receptive.

Saturday, September 5, 1987

How I struggle in my ovulating "all over the place" space. Oh how lovemaking would release and channel energy and focus my being. I miss being married to you, R. I miss being your spouse and friend. I miss you.

Sunday, September 6, 1987

I drive to the county park and walk the beach barefooted on the cool sand. The sound of the water is soothing and healing. Signs of transition to fall surround me in the red-tinged leaves, the cooler sand, the earlier dusk, the smell of the woods awaiting winter's rest. And I join my own transitioning heart to the larger rhythms of the seasons.

Monday, September 7, 1987

I need silence and solitude to acknowledge, feel, and express my sorrow and sadness so I can accept the finality of death and the permanent change this brings. I had to do this internally so Laura doesn't end up carrying it. This is my way of loving her.

I feel spent; my eyes burn, my neck and shoulders feel weary.

I cry out, giving voice to my suffering.

I miss you, R.

I love you.

I wanted to walk with you and grow old with you.

Good-bye, R.

Peace, R.

You are so present; I hear your voice call my name almost as if you wanted to cradle and comfort me. You were so present, big as life, and then you would fade as you walked toward the yellow light:

—walked away from me

—walked toward what would bring you life

Good-bye again, R.

My God, my God, crucified and weary-worn, wounded yet arisen, caress me and heal me this night. I feel needy and so spent. Be with me. Let my sleep and dreams be healing. Re-energize me to be a potent, feeling, wounded woman as I return to work tomorrow. Bless me with your peace which surpasses all understanding. Spirit alive within me, grant me wisdom and strength. I surrender myself weary and worn.

Thursday, September 9, 1987

Dream:

> I am in a lovely church setting with lots of light and windows opening to nature. A woman approaches me. Her face is sacred and dignified. The babushka on her head is pulled forward to shadow her face. There is a beauty and serenity about her; it is evident she has suffered deeply. She confides in me speaking of her self-consciousness.
>
> I am not a priest who can give her absolution but that doesn't seem to matter. Together we pray for healing. She asks me to touch her face. I do, and as we pray her skin becomes smooth and transformed. There are some scars remaining but not the deep convoluted disfigurement.

The disfigured sorrowing part of me reaches out for healing. Is the dream suggesting that I can heal myself?

Saturday, September 12, 1987

Today is six months since R. died—a half of a year. It seems like years in terms of the intensity of the feelings I've felt; it seems like yesterday in terms of how much I miss him; it seems like never in terms of wanting/wishing his return.

How I miss you, R., your goodness, your humor, your spontaneity. How L. misses you, but often cannot directly say. Damn, I get so angry when I think of what she is missing, of what you are missing! Parenting alone is the toughest part. That is where you hung in there the most, even when you withdrew in other ways. I've done most everything else alone—lived alone, maintained a living space, budgeted, paid bills, traveled, decided, vacationed—but not parented. I miss our sense of family so deeply. And I wonder—are you feeling now? Do you see us and care? Are you affected by what you see? I feel a burning sensation in my chest as I love you and ache with you. I struggle so with decisions about Laura, and we have years ahead of us . . .

Sunday, September 13, 1987

I feel like I could cry right now like a little child who wants to be held and patted on the back and reassured that everything will somehow be all right. And yet what I sense and feel is that I must mirror this to my daughter, while creating the safe space for her to go through her pain and grief. Who can hold my child-woman parts and help me to know a oneness?

Monday, September 14, 1987

I need to continue to take care of myself and limit outside involvement. A moratorium of sorts has been very necessary.

Tuesday, September 15, 1987

I go to bed and ask for comfort and consolation. I lie awake remembering R. and feeling the ache of his absence. How I long to be gathered up with all my feelings and just held.

Sunday, September 20, 1987

Tonight I know such an agony, which is deepened by the fatigue of going it alone . . .

Tuesday, September 22, 1987

Today I miss you as my daily companion—the one with whom I break and share bread.

At other times I am almost too weary and stretched to remember and miss you. That is when such numbness could set in . . .

Friday, September 25, 1987

What a difference restful, renewing sleep makes. I am grateful and willing to feel anew . . .

Monday, September 28, 1987

I feel my fear and cry through it to a place of safety. I am afraid to acknowledge that I am a passionate woman with deep desires. That is a part of my very being, despite whether or not I am married or in a relationship with another that provides opportunities for physical intimate expression. The thought of relating with someone new is far too wearying. I trust the unfolding, grateful to have faced a fear.

Saturday, October 3, 1987

This weekend I go to a retreat center in a rustic nature setting to be alone. As welcoming and familiar as this lovely place is, I am gripped by a terror. I realize how worn out and tired I am.

As I walk amidst golden-hued leaves, I am drawn toward a golden pink-red maple. Its leaves are a bouquet of fire. Unlike its neighboring mighty conifer with a singular trunk grounded and rooted deeply, the maple has many trunks with no center of being. It lacked the care of pruning; "natural," if it means untended is not always best. The maple tree, though, symbolized how I was feeling—going off in a number of directions. It was more like a bush than a tree! Its energy was being "given away," if you will, into all the side branches rather than the life-supporting main trunk. It had a beauty all its own but not the serene, solid, centered beauty of a stately, sturdy maple tree.

I don't want to be a bush!
I want to be a maple tree!

That means pruning . . .
> and tending . . .
> and being cared for . . .

That means not just being out in nature in a "natural" state of being.

That means pruning a lot of the branches that drain or divert my energy.

That means being rooted and connected to the Source of Life!

Sunday, October 4, 1987

I am being pruned and stripped, cut to my core. That is the agony I experience.

I let go and give away that of Raymond which still binds me so that I may reclaim my power and bear fruit. I am frightened but trusting.

Monday, October 7, 1987

In my aloneness, I learn anew to ask for help.

Monday, October 12, 1987

After an active, focused day I pause, and at nightfall, weeping enters in . . .

I know R.'s absence, R.'s presence.

Friday, October 16, 1987

I am tired of being tired and so weary.

My whole being aches to be pampered, to rest, to winter.

Instead, so much activity fills these days.

My neck lymph glands are very swollen; my system is fighting infection with all its might!

I grieve and cry, sobbing aloud.

I promised loving for a lifetime. You can't just "turn that off" like a switch when your beloved suddenly dies.

Saturday, October 17, 1987

As I miss the presence of your spirit, I struggle to know the strength of my own spirit.

Sunday, October 18, 1987

I ask for STRENGTH:

—the strength to be still

—the strength to listen

—the strength to be weak

—the strength to risk

—the strength to move forward

—the strength to BE

—the strength to LOVE

only because I am loved.

I give thanks for JOY:

—the joy of knowing I am loved

—the joy of you within me always

—the joy which pain and sorrow do not erase

—the joy of self-knowing

—the joy of truly loving

Tuesday, October 20, 1987

My fear in saying "no" to invitations is connected with the fear that my grieving will not end or change. And yet in saying "no," I say "yes" to me, to L.

Friday, October 30, 1987

I celebrate the specialness of this day, my birthday, by living its ordinariness! Each day is such a celebration of life. Only genuine silence and quiet tears express my soul this night.

Saturday, October 31, 1987

The leaves are falling as they do every year; more trees are bare than not. My days are like this—emerging in an array of colors, displaying themselves quietly and then falling to the ground with little fanfare.

It is Halloween and I miss R.'s jovial, playful way with the kids.

Friday, November 6, 1987

Today I take a mental health day from work. I listened to the funeral tape. Somehow I needed to do this today—to re-feel the intensity of those days without the deep grief. Even my crying is different. Perhaps it is the crying of letting go rather than the crying of loss. This is a more painful and alone letting go of R. than his death. There is no drama; it is internal.

Tuesday, November 10, 1987

How do I redirect the devotion I had toward you, R.?

Wednesday, November 11, 1987

I recall this evening seven years ago and R.'s constant vigil as L. worked her way through my body to be born. Never have I seen R. more deeply touched—at once excited and peaceful.

I fall asleep weeping!

Saturday, November 14, 1987

I feel like a sponge absorbing and absorbing people's pain and hurt and confusion. No wonder I have to "squeeze" so much out through my own tears.

I miss R. in ever-new ways as we celebrate our daughter's birthday and I recall the intimate moments surrounding her birth. People will gather today, and you will not be present. People will leave and you will not be here to debrief with me.

I feel my aloneness these days, an aloneness and thirst for union, a sense of family, making history together that no friendship can fill in the same way. The love and support of friends seem to deepen my capacity to feel my raw pain.

Monday, November 16, 1987

I am so tired. I hurt.

Tuesday, November 17, 1987

I awaken with a dream:

> *There is an informal gathering. Laura says, "How I'd like Daddy to play [his guitar]." I feel R.'s presence*

strongly. He appears beside me. When he is seen by the others, he is invited to play. He walks to center front of room. He is centered, serene, poised and peaceful. I cry and cry, and then cry out: "I love you! I miss you! I am deeply sad for what could have been. I carry you in my heart forever and know your presence." R. says: "Honor your soul, M. Go in; not to do that is to die."

I awaken with tears and a wet pillow.

Wednesday, November 18, 1987
It takes so much energy to go forward without R.

Friday, November 20, 1987
Slowly I begin to feel safe again. I experience safety in the present but get scared when I look ahead. Perhaps I am afraid of what I might discover and where I might be led, quite alone. And so I sleep in surrender and let myself absorb my sadness, my fears, my tiredness, and yet know peace in the midst.

Sunday, November 22, 1987
How I long to be freed from my fears.

Thursday, November 26, 1987
In an ongoing process of letting go, I say good-bye to R. It is like I have made room or a niche for the ache I will always carry within me, instead of constantly experiencing myself as one big ache. I have had to grieve and mourn until R. could dance in my heart. He is there more deeply than I could ever express to anyone! You are in me, R., forever! I miss you on this Thanksgiving Day. I will miss you around our family table. And yet I go to celebrate, knowing a wholeness unto myself. I ache for what could have been and let go over and over, to make room to dream new dreams and walk a path without you, my beloved spouse.

Putting Death to Rest

I have kept one red rose, with its now-faded, darkening petals, on my desk to "feel" its dying. It has spent itself in a burst of deep, energetic beauty and is now blackened with the onset of death. The green feathery ferns have lost their chlorophyll—that life-light substance—and instead of black, bear the yellowed, sallow color of death.

I have welcomed the rose and watched it changing. Now it is time to put it to rest. The rose stands as a symbol of "putting death to rest"—putting Raymond's death to rest. We put R.'s body "to rest" in the cemetery on March 16th, but grieving and mourning needed to happen before we could put R.'s death to rest.

The rose dies as we await the winter equinox. I think about what roses do at these times of wintering,their branches pruned to the core. They rest. They gather energy for new life and growth. Their darkened petals and dried leaves are long gone. Death has been put to rest . . .

Saturday, November 28, 1987

I celebrate more and more that everything matters because nothing matters except loving. To love until I die of loving . . .

Monday, November 30, 1987

Last night I spontaneously chose to watch an evening movie—a testimony to the power and strength of love. This is the first evening TV movie I've watched since R.'s death. I have moved alone through yet one more thing which we enjoyed doing together.

Tuesday, December 1, 1987

Today the car is in need of major repairs, and practical tasks that we shared now burden me alone. I ache again that we didn't have the kind of insurance which would pay off our home mortgage in the event of death. And yet, for some reason, this burden is now part of my path.

Monday, December 7, 1987

I believe that R. and I will meet again with joy and gladness, that sorrow and mourning will flee. And yet, meanwhile, dearest one, beloved spouse and father, son and friend, companion on this journey of life, meanwhile, R., you dance in my heart, and that enables me to carry the hope . . .

Sunday, December 13, 1987

I hear someone speak of the four chambers of the heart. I imagine R.'s heart—tiring and overworking those last months, and finally bursting, exploding with fatigue. And I ache. This ache is ever deeper than the pain that precipitates crying. And so I move through the ninth month. Since R.'s death, I move into a place to which I cannot give voice.

Tuesday, December 15, 1987

My heart burns with a holding fire; I am cradled and held by a love beyond all knowing. Please heal my broken heart.

Saturday, December 19, 1987

Holiday vacation begins, and I feel my aloneness in this transition space. I am not as afraid as I am sad. I enjoy sharing my life on a daily basis. R.'s dying and death deprive me of that opportunity. And friendship, by its nature, does not allow for that in terms of frequency, dailyness, and spontaneity—unless one was to live with a friend, sharing space and table and time.

I sit in the family room cuddling L., just looking at the tree. Memories come racing across every limb, but no longer tears, only an ache and sadness—a sense of something precious and unfolding—our life together—being cut off. I grieve and feel the loss as acutely as if a body part had been amputated.

As I write holiday cards, I find myself feeling unsettled regarding my friendship with men. These established friendships endured through my marriage. Will my expression of affection be received in a different light now that I am no longer married?

Monday, December 21, 1987

There is something awesome and scary about facing the future. I'm embarking on a path with a new sense of aloneness. Sometimes I am too tired to cry even though my weary body longs for release.

Tuesday, December 22, 1987

In my remembering today, I connect with parts of myself that remain unreceived. My tears begin to be for me!

Thursday, December 24, 1987

With what deep and unspeakable fullness I know and continue to desire rebirth.

I weep but maybe it is really a "we" as my thoughts turn to the many who are hurting, alone, missing someone. I hold them close and, yes, "we" weep.

Friday, December 25, 1987

Today I cry with others in missing you. I feel your absence acutely as we celebrate the traditions of this season without you.

Tuesday, December 29, 1987

As I look out at the winter landscape I feel such sadness and some anger. I feel a sense of being deserted by R. How could you leave L. and me? How could you miss out on all the goodness of these days?

Wednesday, December 30, 1987

Today I so longed for another chance with R., to work things out, to celebrate the rhythm of the seasons, to grow old together.

Your parents talk about you as a young boy; there is so much that will go unlived, dearest R. Damn, I miss you! With what longing I desire to be embraced by you, to hug and hold you, to kiss you with the passion of a spouse!

How I longed to love you wholeheartedly, devotedly, faithfully! I feel so cheated—only eight and a half short years— enough to begin to know each other, discover the tough spots, but never really reap the harvest of our loving. Why, oh why?!?

Even if I could answer the "why," it wouldn't change the dailyness; it wouldn't fill the void left by your absence. No one/other can! You are forever indelibly part of me, R. I love you and I miss loving you!

I have ended and begun the last ten years with R. I miss being married, yet have no desire for remarriage. I don't feel like starting over. I do want to love and be loved.

As a new year lies before us, I feel scared to really feel all my fears.

How I wanted to love you well, R.! How I wanted to grow old with you! How I wanted to be with you anew when L. grew and left home, and we could recapture the spontaneity and privacy of our early days. How I wanted to struggle with you, learn from you and with you! How I wanted to celebrate your successes! Oh, R., I sob and sob in wanting to reach out and touch you so. In our darkest times together, I never once gave up hope for us. I would get discouraged and feel so broken, but I never despaired. I loved you in a way I've never loved anyone, R. And the hurt of missing you is unlike anything I've felt.

I was feeling that I had touched the deepest depths and felt the sharpest pain, but I have not yet wintered without you, R. Your spirit is everywhere and in me so.

Tonight my deepest desire is to be with you, R., to hold each other tenderly, to stroke your beard, have you lick my breasts and kiss with passionate pressure. Then to lay side-by-side and talk and dream. And then maybe you'd get up, get your guitar, and sing me a song. Come and visit me in my dreams this night, R. How I long to communicate with you in some way! How I long for some response, for some way of knowing that you hear, that you feel, that you still love me, that somehow you too miss me and desire our bonding and reuniting.

Friday, January 1, 1988

I am glad to be alive on this first morning of a new year awaiting the dawn and welcoming the year with hope!

Tuesday, January 5, 1988

Your father dies suddenly, R. I am so unready to meet this so soon after losing you.

Wednesday, January 6, 1988

In my tears of yesterday's knowing, I cry out, "I'm not ready for this!" and I'm not . . .

Thursday, January 7, 1988

R., where are you? I want to know your presence, and yet I go alone, feeling my aloneness anew, with feelings of grief and loss and mourning.

I feel so weak and little and vulnerable, so raw and open and wounded. I am afraid of being broken.

Friday, January 8, 1988

My eyes burn when I awaken, feeling as if I have been sobbing. I feel a sense of some release and relief.

We buried my father-in-law today. A deeply renewed ache accompanies my exhaustion. I feel like a little girl who had fallen, received lots of scrapes and bruises that had scabbed over and were healing. Then I fell again and all the scabs were ripped off, wounds re-opened and oozing. I get back on the bike to continue riding, but the going is slower and very painful. I hurt and ache.

Tuesday, January 12, 1988

Today is ten months since you died.

I would like to write at length, but my weariness is overpowering and the demands of the day call me.

Wednesday, January 13, 1988

Today I give myself permission to hold my feelings, to feel and cry when I'm ready, so as, perhaps, to move into a time when I won't cry.

Later, I want to reach out and feel what I'm feeling with someone. I am raw and weary from my tears. I try calling friends for support. No answer . . . I am alone and cry to sleep.

Friday, January 14, 1988

I am wound up after a full week. How I would enjoy making love right now—to be in my body, to be bodily, to express the depth of what has been stirred up in me.

Monday, January 18, 1988

I feel my aloneness, letting the evening quiet envelop me, choosing not to watch TV.

I continue to have so many practical items with which to deal. Tax time approaches and so a new hurdle. And yet the more I can verbalize what I need and want, the more I know support in letting it happen.

Tuesday, January 19, 1988

I feel beaten and weary after a stressful day at work. I miss debriefing with you, R.

Thursday, January 21, 1988

Today, rather spontaneously, I decide to clean out and reorganize some drawers. Caught unawares, I come to the top dresser drawer with all of R.'s odds and ends. There are miscellaneous receipts, a shirt ruffle and bow tie, a pen with his initials, some rock fossils, his camping knife. I store these in a small box. Two bottles of cologne and a new box of condoms remain. Somehow I have to deal with those things ritually later.

I come across a scribbled note which R. wrote in December before he died. We had gone to a wedding together. R. wore his new striped suit. We held hands during the ceremony and silently renewed our own vows. I understand what it means to be heartbroken. I ache with the pain of dashed hopes and unlived dreams. I miss the give and take of marriage, difficult and demanding as it sometimes was. I miss loving R. I miss making love. I miss you, R.! I miss the ordinariness and spontaneity. I miss the debates and discussions about our next purchase. I miss delighting in our daughter with you! I miss remembering those parts of our past together. I miss your laugh. I miss hearing you call me "Meig." I miss a call from you at work. I miss calling you at lunch and expressing my desire to make love, to pleasure you.

My cries of "Why?" are gradually replaced by feeling, by letting grief be. Initially the cries of "Why?" seemed to ask as if an answer would take away the pain, or if I knew "why," then it would be less painful. Awareness doesn't ease or erase the pain. It does deepen the loneliness of the pain.

And I find that as people around me forget, I need to remember. In one sense I will never tire of talking of and remembering R. for I am changed forever.

Sunday, January 24, 1988

Throughout the day my thoughts return to the idea of partnership, especially as it is experienced in marriage. As I listen to other couples together making decisions about their future, I am struck anew by how solitary my journey is. (I am a friend, continuing to know the wrenching that occurs when friends move, and those bonds must be maintained across distances with infrequent physical proximity.) My partner through eight-and-a-half years of marriage is dead. This morning I dreamed of his charred skin. I alone must create new life from the ashes.

My deepest longings and yearnings to journey with another were most poignantly expressed in my wedding vows—the promise to journey with another day in and day out, to grow old together, to comfort one another, to be for and with one another. R.'s death, unlike anything I've experienced, teaches me how to grieve and mourn and know loss, letting it touch every fiber of my being. I am being changed with each registered feeling, each remembered joy, each tear.

Tuesday, January 26, 1988

Some mornings all I can think about is being back in bed. I am so exhausted and feel so vulnerable.

Friday, January 29, 1988

I dream about arid, controversial land through which I'm hesitant to travel, and yet it is the only way to the mountain. I pause, and then I hear: "feel everything, Margaret, but let it flow from your center." I image a gurgling, grounded fountain within me. Then consciously choose to express/release it in some way.

Sunday, January 31, 1988

When I feel depressed, I usually want to get out of it; that is freeing and promotes movement.

When I feel sadness, I want to experience it, to meet it, not to avoid it. I want to cry and feel the depths I am knowing. Sadness, like love, enables me to see in a new way.

The sadness I am knowing is not without hope; it has something beautiful and expansive about it. It is an opening, a getting-in-touch. I don't feel a depressed, down-in-the-dumps sadness. This is the kind of sadness I will let run its course, percolating through me to a new stillness.

Friday, February 5, 1988

Each day, with each passing moment, I miss R. from a new space, as I come to know myself in new ways. That is why the hurt continues . . .

Saturday, February 6, 1988

I awaken with this dream:

> *I am at a professional workshop. R. is there, visible only to me. He looks professor-like in his attire. His face is emaciated and reflects a death-like mask. He is cold to the touch. I talk to him, so glad he is there. He tells me, "I'm dead, Margaret." Then I move into the presenter space previously occupied by R. I easily answer questions; the answers flow from a knowing space within me. I have the sense that I have carried a dream for R. NOW—live it!*

Sunday, February 7, 1988

Yesterday R.'s niece was married. I stood tall and was potently present to each moment, each feeling, each person.

I felt regal in my aloneness, able to carry myself with a sense of self. I cried during the service several times, feeling the pain of not being married to R., feeling the pain of his absence beside me, remembering our wedding day.

I cried from a place of healing and lightness as well, knowing as I move forward that paradoxically death parted us and yet even death can't part us now. I am reclaiming parts of R. more and more. I know that I have loved, have been loved, and continue to love another.

Tuesday, February 9, 1988

I feel the lack of depth in my breathing and the energy drain that happens when I can't take in air; it is as if I can't take in life deeply. My chest is weeping, and I long to cry out my grief.

Sunday, February 14, 1988

I just ache and know such unspeakable grief. Nothing satisfies—not companionship or reading or exercise.

I sense my grief and sadness are coming from such a deep place that it is taking time to surface and emerge and be expressed. It is so difficult to balance this internal process with the external demands. I am so tired of balancing.

Monday, February 15, 1988

It takes such courage to grieve!

Friday, February 19, 1988

The descent is the prelude to rebirth, new life!
It is slow. I ask for patience.
It is painful. I ask for courage to feel.
It is terrifying. I ask for safety.

Sunday, February 21, 1988

Dream:

> *I spot R.'s car parked at the curb. He is wearing his navy prestige suit. I greet him; we are in the front seat. He embraces me and we kiss passionately, communicating a depth without words. Oh, how I've missed you, R.*

Today's scripture reading invites us to "Reform . . ." I thought of how I have had to re-form because of R.'s death:

—re-form my sense of identity

—re-form sense of family

—re-form ways of parenting

—re-form dreams and goals

I miss you, R. I miss debriefing with you. I miss loving you. I miss mirroring to each other. I miss your laugh and your humor. I miss your grandiosity. I miss your music. I miss your soul. I miss you!

Thank you for visiting me in my dreams this morning. I am struck by the movements over these past months—from your dying, as I witness your peaceful walk toward a yellow light, through dreams of death masks and cold skin to the connective rebirth of passionate, wordless embracing.

Friday, February 27, 1988

Today I cried and walked. My tears are cries of anguish, not anger or despair, but hurt—from a deep space of woundedness. I want to be with someone who appreciated R.'s spirit. I need/want a hug. I contact J., R.'s friend, who is willing to be with me. I just sob. J. understands R.'s specialness and the specialness of a first love. I am able to verbalize the depth of the bond which I continue to know with Raymond. I love him so, and my love endures! When I tell J. of dreams, he asks, "How is R.?" I feel connected and received by J. I thank him; I appreciate him because he too loved R.

Wednesday, March 2, 1988

I have focused so much on emotional turmoil that today I had to relearn physical sickness. I have the flu. I observe some differences between physical illness and emotional weakness.

Physical Illness/Sickness	Emotional Weakness
Σ feel bodily ache	Σ feel heart and soul
Σ slow motion	Σ selective slow motion (example, work)
Σ can be mentally alert but body weak	Σ can feel confused and overwhelmed but body strong
Σ physical exercise unappealing	Σ physical exercise appealing
Σ little energy for writing/reflection	Σ lots of energy for writing/reflection

Tuesday, March 8, 1988

Today I miss R. and how he expressed his soul through music. I feel deep pain and sorrow for my nonacceptance of him at times. How I want another chance.

It is so easy to get bogged down in being overwhelmed by the whole! I want to be strengthened in the will to live!

Part Three: DAWN

"[Our sadnesses] are the moments

when something new had entered

into us, something unknown; our feelings

grow mute in shy perplexity, everything

in us withdraws, a stillness comes,

and the new, which no one knows,

stands in the midst of it and is

silent."

—Rainer Maria Rilke, *Letters to a Young Poet*

The darkness which ensues following the death of a loved one feels like an imprisonment. There is no escaping it. The loss frames every experience. There is a need and desire for liberation.

As the tree stump is removed, shredded and reunited with the soil of the earth, something dead is returned and renewed, making room for new life. There is still the void of where the tree grew; its missing presence can be haunting. Yet in the new, fertile soil, nourished by the tears of suffering, some new shoots may sprout.

I held my husband's hand as he died and spoke to him of my presence and love. "I'm here, Raymond. I am with you." I sensed his spirit separating from the body I held and was aware of a yellow light. We walked toward its inviting glow. And then I could go no further. R. had to walk on alone. It was at this moment that I knew he had walked on to "the other side," long before I was told he had died. The darkness of his pain and suffering and incompleteness had been transformed into the dawn of a new way of being.

I traveled memories and voids, remembered a love, and cried a loss. It took me a long year to reach that place of dawn. Within the vessel of my own being, having confronted the darkness of death, I began to have a heart and the eyes to see the glimmers of dawn.

Part Three contains journal entries written during the second year after R.'s death. My world, disoriented by the darkness of loss, now takes on a hopeful glow in the dawn's light. My world was shattered in a moment. In the dawn's light, I gain strength to continue the repair. I walk into the dawn alone.

Giving Voice to Hope

Saturday, March 12, 1988—one year anniversary of R.'s death

I watch some video tapes of R. I am amazed anew and delight in R.'s creativity. I mourn the loss of his gifts to me and to the world. I acknowledge my deep sorrow in being "cheated" of the opportunity to grow with R. and learn from him. At the same time I celebrate the awareness that I now carry those R. parts for myself. And as I reclaim them, R. does live on more fully.

This day marks a remembering of pain and loss and yet also relief—I can stop counting, marking each twelfth of the month. I embrace and live the feelings and then re-experience anew the forgetting. More and more, at deeper and deeper levels, I will carry R.'s memory and the pain of his loss alone.

I reflect on how clearly I was thinking at the time of R.'s death. I was feeling and functioning, making choices and saying what I wanted, asking for help practically and emotionally. Grace was definitely operating and continues to aid me. I was able to be in touch with my deepest parts because I was connected to one greater than I, embracing all. I was able to receive from a deeper spirit, all-wise and all-embracing, because I was connected at my center. Is this all one and the same—an expression of the divine within us?!?

There is a deeper knowing part of me—that space beyond pain and pleasure. Again and again, alone and in silence, I meet all that pains and puzzles me, moving beyond the loss to a space of indescribable quiet.

I have been impoverished by R.'s death, by his physical parting! And the tears I am crying are for me. I feel sorrow at losing out on ways of growing and loving. I witness the pain of L.'s emptiness in being cheated of knowing her father as she grows into a woman. I have felt poverty this past year. Perhaps

that is why my body, soul and spirit desire the plenitude of play
this summer.

I feel. That almost breaks me. I suffer and grope for a way of
dealing with it.

As I've allowed myself to feel, I have known pain and joy,
ecstasy and agony; I've laughed and cried; I've loved and
suffered. That is all part of the "groping."

I sorrow over distance from R., even as I deeply know a bond
of love. In being wounded and allowing myself to feel, suffer,
receive, and be healed, I come to know a new quiet strength.

Sunday, March 13, 1988

A light dusting of snow has fallen, and a few flurries still
dance.

Living Spirit, Eternal Lover, thank you for the strength to feel
and be present, to honor R., to express my soul. I know the desire
of a lover to be with the beloved. I know the longing of a lover to
embrace. I know the satisfaction of a lover to be still in oneness.
In knowing this, I believe I know you. The gratitude I know for
the journey of this past year is beyond words. You, Divine Lover,
continue to be my constant companion, loving me to a space
beyond pain and pleasure—even as I intensely experience each.

Thursday, March 17, 1988

Physical symptoms of stuffiness and congestion seem to
manifest my heavy heart—heavy in the remembering of these
past five days a year ago. A new year has begun; but there is
nothing magical. The ache must take its own time. This day
simply invites me to take another step forward.

Sunday, March 20, 1988

When I focus on R., I miss him, yet I know that he is at peace
and unburdened of the heaviness of his deep wounds. I trust, I
know, I understand. He lives within me, and I live within him
beyond what words can convey. He lives in me when I think out
loud, laugh heartily, delight in L., pause to enjoy music, play
before tasks are compulsively completed, write to express my
soul.

And I, too, live within you, R. Somehow my loving and accepting you has made a difference. No words can fully speak of that love—a love that joined despite our differences and wounds. And so when I cry, when I weep, I am feeling and expressing the pain of those words unspoken forever.

I hear you inviting me to love myself, inviting me to self-care. This will enable me to love L., to keep your memory close, and to be open to the best of everything.

I can't walk in the world for you, R.

I can only walk for myself.

Thank you for releasing me to walk in the world for me.

I know I need to write. I need to mold into a "sculpture" all the rough "clay" I have collected. If and when I can write of R. for the public, I will have said good-bye and moved forward—walking for myself . . .

I feel my aloneness and know that the state of being single as a widow is deeper than a change in a societal role. Yes, I was R.'s wife, but that was only one aspect of my identity. It's like I've pulled that "spoke" back now—the one that publicly and radically expressed a commitment to love and grow with one man. Even when our relating was rocky and my hopes dashed, there was a calming strength and a strengthening calm in the knowledge that I was married/wedded/committed. That is gone now in the outer, and yet I am not single in the same previous way. I am single now, having been spouse, having loved and been loved; and that makes all the difference in the world!

Thursday, March 31, 1988
Dream:

> *R. driving a car with children in it. I am driving a car, traveling behind him. At one point we stop; R. has been gone and wants to come back. I embrace him, yet know there is no turning back.*

Friday, April 1, 1988
It is difficult to walk on alone.

Saturday, April 2, 1988

I know a deep, quiet joy and a deep sense of being loved by a love that is stronger, much stronger, than death. That alone enables me to choose life even as I know such anguish of spirit, and love forevermore with a broken, wounded heart which has been stretched and deepened.

Sunday, April 10, 1988

Today would have been R.'s fortieth birthday. I awaken with this dream:

> R. has decided to sell his car (not a trade-in); he
> won't need it anymore . . .
> I drive it for the last time to work.

Sunday, May 22, 1988

Love is longing and waiting, for love longs to be fulfilled. Love-longing . . . With longing I continue to love you, R., until we meet again in a new life.

Sunday, May 28, 1988

I watch a program concerning the Vietnam Veterans' Memorial. Remembering is so key to knowing ourselves in the present.

I remember you, R. I miss you. This is a night when a shared history with another means so much: to talk and to "walk" together the journey of remembering . . . And then to entwine wordlessly and make love, together celebrating something larger than either of our individual stories . . .

Wednesday, June 2, 1988

I remember, and yet with each passing day your memory fades. There is more and more distance between when I last touched you and now, between when I last told you "I love you" and now, between when I last felt your smile and now, between when I last heard your voice and the stark emptiness of your absence now. There are times I still wait for you to walk through the door or sit at the table with us.

Friday, June 3, 1988
>   With wordless love
>   I hold you in smiling, silent embrace
>   wiping tears
>   touching smile lines
>   comforting
>   knowing an all-embracing love
>   I hold and am
>   woman-lover

Saturday, June 4, 1988
>   R. fades within me in some ways and deepens within me in other ways . . . And truly, I continue to grow in loving him across barriers of time, space, death. I embrace him with a silent wordless love!

Sunday, June 12, 1988
>   I pictured R. alive and laughing, but no more.
>   I pictured R. in the coffin, cold to my touch.
>   Something is being completed in me regarding R.'s death. Last night was the first time I socialized with couples since R. died. Although I was "uncoupled," so to speak, I felt comfortable and enjoyed myself.
>   Mellowed and strengthened by pain and tears, I wipe away the tears and know with R. a bond of wordless love—a love that is stronger than death.

Thursday, June 16, 1988
>   It is as if the chapter entitled "The Wounded Widow" is drawing to a close. And I am opening the chapter entitled "The Wounded Woman." My aloneness overpowers me. I feel confused and needy.

Tuesday, July 19, 1988
>   I feel the emptiness of your spontaneous presence. As I move into new spaces of letting go, I could have appreciated R. in new ways.

Sunday, August 7, 1988
   There are days I still think your death isn't forever.

Sunday, August 14, 1988
   Today I had the space, courage, and energy to sort through some of R.'s boxes in the basement. I was deeply saddened as I fingered the many expressions of his spirit and creativity. I ache deeply in feeling my limitedness, which R. complemented, especially through musical and artistic expression.
   The weeping fig tree, a funeral plant, continues to lose its leaves—letting go, almost as if it was silently weeping, exposing here and there bare branches.

Friday, August 15, 1988
   I have been accustomed to swallowing feelings and emotions without assimilating them. Assimilating requires struggling and wrestling as I am now doing.

Sunday, August 28, 1988
   I deeply feel my aloneness this evening.
   Tonight is a night for making love, for being caught up in mystery and rapture—not to escape but to feel, not to tune out but to gain perspective.
   I experience my aloneness anew, so wanting daily sharing.

Friday, September 2, 1988
   Again my feelings lie too deep for tears!
   Something is dying and ending in me today—what would have been our tenth wedding anniversary, and almost eighteen months since R.'s death.
   How I wanted to grow old with you, R., to learn from your complementary ways, to delight in our daughter together, let her go and then "re-meet" as lovers alone. I loved you! And I miss you deeply.
   I ask you to love me from afar and channel strength and wisdom toward me, so I can go forward from a knowing space. I came to know how much I loved you—so much that I let go and

honored your choice even as I deeply grieve your loss, R. And I have this sense that you "feel" some sadness of incompleteness. I sense you suffer in the deepest parts of your loving heart when you see Laura's pain in missing you. And I sense your heart as well when you see my pain and agony. I am very bonded to you and with you this day, R., these days . . . forever!

It is now late and I weep from a deep space, feeling the hollow that will forever be.

Friday, October 28, 1988

I prepare to remove you, fig tree, from the study, my sacred at-home space. You have been a symbol of new life since R.'s death. A gift of his colleagues, you symbolized the fruits that were not to be borne in R.'s life. Your graceful greenness buoyed my spirit many a morning. Gradually I pruned your withered branches to direct the life-energy toward the still green area. But ever so slowly you withered. You remind me poignantly that I too am dying and will die. My life here has a span, a beginning and an end. Someone will bury me as I will return you to the earth today. Thank you for your life and your death, and the gift of your dying. Thank you for teaching me anew of the rhythms of this journey of our earthbound life. As your spirit is reunited with the soil of the earth, something is returned and renewed and "makes room" for new life. Your missing presence, oh little fig tree, will add a new simplicity to my sacred space. I will not replace you with a new plant or another fig tree. Your lifetime and gift to me were uniquely your own. I have learned and been blessed and now journey on to learn anew. I return you now to the glorious woods which lie in winter readiness. Thank you! You have loved me well and graced my dwelling by your being.

December 3, 1988

I just finished watching a holiday concert. The wind roars outside, and I am full in missing you, R. Your spirit was so present in the music, and I miss bantering with you in such soul moments. There is little to say or write; how I would enjoy making love with passionate energy and deep passion . . .

February 17, 1989

I am even more connected to R. as I own my own power as a woman. I ache in knowing that I will not be sharing that growth with him, my beloved and spouse, in a daily, unfolding way. And yet our connectedness only deepens. Having loved and been loved in a committed, faithful, spousal way enables me to go to the depths of solitude, feeling and being with myself in ways that this alone enables. I am moving into a new space of being at one with myself.

Part Four: DAYLIGHT

. . . the exquisite "pain of love"

simply is

an inescapable part of its

power.

—Robert Moore and Douglas Gillette

Emerging from the darkness that surrounds and imprisons the grieving of a loved one alters our way of seeing. Our eyes have to adjust to a brighter light. As they do, we are able to see the simple and ordinary in new ways.

Once a tree has been uprooted, the stump removed, and the ground prepared anew, it is possible to imagine the space holding something other than the former tree. Yet somehow the memory of the tree—its shape, size, scent, changing colors—is still present.

The grief which I know never ends; it only changes as it fills an ever quieter, deeper space accessible only to me. As the months and years move on, I feel detached and separate from R.'s dying, which is now in me as part of my history.

I know and come to accept that I will not be free of the pain of loss. As light fills my days and softens the initial darkness which imprisoned me, I learn to live with the pain, knowing that I am forever different. My hopes died with R., but somehow in the writing of my journey since his death, I am re-kindling new ones. Slowly, in the light of day, I walk forward on my own path without R.

Part Four contains journal entries from the second anniversary of R.'s death through two more years. There is an integrating of the experience of loss that enables me to make new choices. And yet as a new ordinariness sets in, I find significant events still trigger tears of remembrance. They subside but do not disappear.

I have become accustomed to missing R. I dare to live in the present without him, boldly going forward into the light.

Giving Voice to Courage

March 12, 1989—second anniversary of R.'s death.
I awaken with this dream:

> *I am at a conference. I am there with R. and three other women. R. and I have separate rooms. I want the chance to be together and picture myself gently making love, stroking R.'s face, kissing him, being entered by him and gently being as one. R.'s shoes are in my room. I gather them and take them to his room as we pack to prepare to leave. He says he doesn't have room in his suitcase. I leave the room to continue packing.*

Even as I dream this, I know R. is dead. This is not a flashback. I feel present, a nowness. Perhaps it is simply commenting on the longing I experience and the unfinishedness I know with R. His shoes, a symbol of grounding and a foundation, are in my room. I return them. I must stand on my own two feet alone.

I feel emptied; something has again gone out of me. I am no longer using energy to love, accept, and hang-in there with R. That challenge is over. I am no longer wife in the outer sense.

The date-memory seems to bring so much back. I feel thrown back into a space of re-healing. I feel weakened in the process, yet more centered. Dreaming my longing and desire somehow allows me to go down into the hurt and move through it.

It is time to dry my tears.

March 25, 1989
I know a sense of the finality of my separation from R., a letting go.

As I reclaim my own parts, R. dearest, I release you to be free, alone and at one. I have wept deeply for what will never be; it is now time to dry my tears.

I release the past.
I go forward in love.
I am free to move forward with love in my heart.

April 9, 1989

The agony of the aloneness
of grieving
rips at my core and surfaces tears too long kept

No one can ever know how I loved R.,
(I don't know if he did . . .)
how I cherished his uniqueness
how we made love
how he touched me

I haven't watched a movie at night alone.
That was one of our fond togethernesses—a being with,
feeling, letting go in tears or laughter . . .

We sat apart usually—comfortably separate
Then after the movie we would go upstairs and lie together.

Even in the often-distance, in our apartness,
I harbored the hope that we would grow together;
and as I grew to accept R. more and more for who he was,
my hope seemed to deepen.
So also my aloneness

From the aloneness
of hoping
to—the agony of the aloneness
of grieving.

April 10, 1989

Today would have been R.'s forty-first birthday. My love for him burns within me like an eternal flame. Jackie Kennedy concretized it in a symbol on John's grave. I carry it within me—forever changed by that loving—going out from me and received by me. I weep no longer for R. I have a profound sense of him being at peace—that he finally rests in the arms of a God who can truly hold and embrace all of him. I do continue to feel terrible sadness at what has been lost to the wind, never to be experienced by us. And yet, this is accompanied by a deepening acceptance of what is.

The agony of the aloneness of grieving is an agony one can only experience alone. In and through it surfaces the pleading request to be delivered from such stripping sorrow. And with each tear, each resounding wail, what deepens is only the knowing that this will not be removed. The choice presents: to feel, to know the agony, to be in it, and move through it to acceptance, or to block, deny, busy, and flee the aloneness of the agony and the agony of the aloneness. I am humbly grateful for the strength and courage as well as weakness and fear that have accompanied my choice to enter in. I am part of something larger and am sustained by One who is all-embracing, holding those parts and feelings I sometimes cannot, gently inviting me to open a little more to healing love.

April 26, 1989

Has a great deal which was lived out in relationship now become a part of my potential?

It is time to let go of R., even to put his ghost to rest. As I mourn, R. becomes an "inner figure" and I take back what he carried, as well as discover myself anew without the burden of what he couldn't or wouldn't.

A great deal has been taken away from me in R.'s dying and the resulting separation; however, a great deal is also being given to me. The gifts and blessings in no way negate the pain, the exhaustion, the disruption that R.'s death has brought. Rather, in the very process of entering into these and being scourged and tormented and hollowed out, so to speak, I know a greater, deeper fullness. It is my process, my experience, and may be what I've done most alone in one sense—in terms of what has been transformed in the crucible of my being.

May 3, 1989

These days, like a newly hatched chick or an emerging butterfly, I experience the tiredness of transformation.

May 17, 1989

Today I begin to own some new dreams and plans for myself, of which R. will not be a part.

May 25, 1989

My dream confirms a letting go. I'm carrying my own creativity forward.

> *I'm working in an innovative school setting. On this particular day, when I awaken, R. is in my double bed. I ask what he is doing there; it's too late for this now. I'm moving forward.*

Something has been clarified and deepened in me today. The "how" is still so scary and mysterious but I do trust that this will unfold if I continue to take at least a step!

July 4, 1989

Rilke's words express all I can write today: "WHOM WILL YOU CRY TO, HEART?" (from "Lament").

July 5, 1989

I long for him now, as a widow longs—without expectation.

July 21, 1989

I rewatch *Camelot* and get in touch with the Arthur, Guinevere and Lancelot parts within me. I resonate with each of them, as they say good-bye. I feel moved to drive out to the cemetery. I stop at R.'s grave and tell him of my desire to live and to grow old. Good-bye, my love.

August 1, 1989

Finding some cards which R. and I had written to each other, I sob from a deep soul space. At ever deeper levels, I let go of R., of being his wife and lover, spouse and friend. Somehow my grief work of the past two years is enabling me to do some sorting and reordering in my home. This seems key to making room for something new.

August 5, 1989

The weather today somehow reminds me of R.'s funeral day. I dream of a funeral setting, and as I awaken, I hear, "It is finished." I listen to a bit of the cassette tape from R.'s funeral. I hear with new ears the words which I spoke to our family and friends inviting them to celebrate R.'s life:

"The joy will not replace our deep grief
but will help us make room for new life."

The tape sticks after the word "help," and I smile at the synchronicity, especially in light of this morning's dream.

I release you, only to ever be with you, R. And I go forward choosing to make room for new life.

I walk the summer evening path, release R., and have a deep sense of his peace.

September, 2, 1989

Eleven years ago today, R. and I celebrated our wedding day.

I proceeded to the cemetery this afternoon with the petals from two white roses which have spent their blooms, and ashes from letters which I burned. R. and I wrote the letters expressing our struggles for growth, our confusions, our insecurities, our hopes. I burn them because I know healing in our relating. I feel a joy even as I know a deep ache. Healing has occurred for me, for R., for us and between us. I feel connected to him as a source of strength on "the other side" . . .

We each walk our own path, having walked together for a time. I miss him and cry tears too deep for spilling. I flash to images of sea lions and whales from the ocean depths in my dreams. I am knowing at such new depths and therein touch my aloneness.

From these depths, from this base of healing, I know an energy connection; R. does dance in my heart, and I love him with an everlasting love. I bury these white rose petals and letter ashes near his grave as I begin to experience the emerging phoenix within me rising from the ashes laid by grief and mourning. Every letting go is a burning of sorts. Form and substance are changed; energy remains constant, yet changes forms toward new life! I welcome that building, emerging life and embrace myself and my life in new ways.

I approach the earth. I stand before the noble tree and pray to be reverent as I give thanks. I bury the ashes and the rose petals, letting go of my dreams with R. for our life together . . . and I speak—"R., I love you with an everlasting love!"

September 3, 1989
Something went out of me yesterday and I know it so alone.

September 17, 1989
I miss R. and the chance to work on a committed, permanent relationship.

October 29, 1989
I have been sick with a strep throat and fever. As I feel more rested and a little less weak, I still have little energy to feel, reflect, and process. I feel broken and beaten, and in a state of collapse. I need to feel and experience this state of "collapse" and then rebuild anew, reconstructing myself. This process must be expressing itself in my repeat dreams of a construction project.

Today I know the grief of simply encountering and accepting my own limits, weakness, frailty. My spirit is crushed, my heart is broken. I need to feel my brokenness, to go down and weep, that then I may rebuild anew. Symbolically, it is as if an earthquake or hurricane has occurred within me, leaving me crushed and broken. I can know a certain exhilaration in simply choosing to be gentle with myself.

November 2, 1989
As I sat still briefly this morning, I imagined my broken, depleted spirit as a wounded bird. With wounded left wing, the bird shivers near some still warm ashes that could be fanned into a warming flame. Yet the bird doesn't seem to be able to muster the strength to do it for herself. I stay with the image and feel!

The wounded bird is lying on its wounded left wing in a protective mode. To its right lie some warm ashes; there appears to be devastation all around. (I so want to fan ashes into a flame of heat, warmth, light.)

The bird begins gently flapping its right wing up and down. It is not enough to stir the ashes, but enough to keep the bird's heart beating. (I must first turn inward and kindle the internal flame.)

The wounded bird is so alone, wanting cradling with no arms to comfort her. (Must I somehow muster the energy and strength to fan my own flame, wounded as I am?)

Then, crying inner tears, I become the bird—a fledgling. (I am wounded, yes—scarred on my heart, yet these wings offer new feathers for flight.) The right wing moves up and down freely with energy. The left one is still weak and wet, not unfurled. I can fly to the mountain top, but not yet; my left wing is not ready. I am still out of balance. (Ever slowly, ever gently, I must fan the flame within me so that my spirit will be enlivened and I will be ready for flight. I have been busy using my right wing to try and fan the embers left from the devastation out there. If I pay heed to what is in here, in me, my flame will burn and produce a light that enlivens.)

December 7, 1989

I dream:

> *I seem to be going back and forth across a foreign border. I need to find an apartment. R. seems to be around, or somehow in the picture, yet I don't sense we will be sharing the apartment. It is rather as if he is present, whole and separate, and we are not connected in the outer realm at all. Then R. and I are briskly walking with several other people—a continuously moving group—across the border from East Germany. There are no guards, no fences, no barbed wire; simply a smiling border patrol. We walk with confidence and a spring in our step. R. seems so stately and light on his feet. He is well and at peace. I don't feel the projective urgings which he stirred in me once. I don't feel the triggered pain which being with him at times stirred up. I feel separate. We could re-meet and get to know each other all over again anew.*

December 17, 1989

Tonight I watch "With C. S. Lewis Through the Shadowlands." I feel deeply throughout, and then at the end, when they gave the date C.S. Lewis died and was united with his beloved wife, I weep. I know such a distance and separateness with R. that paradoxically enables the depth of the bond at unspeakable levels.

Somehow in watching this film and having the emotions I did, I know that healing has occurred, and that my grief, pain and hurt have been worked through and are mine. I am no longer experiencing them in their pure rawness.

March 11, 1990

As I cried yesterday, thinking about R., I am aware that I don't grieve on a personal level as much. I have lost a deep sense of identity in no longer being a spouse who is committed to fostering a relationship! I continue to grieve this deeply, wanting to grow old with another.

March 12, 1990—third anniversary of R.'s death

In some senses, simply another day . . .

In one way it is and at the same time, it is a date which marks a love and deep loss for me.

I still sometimes find myself wondering "what if?" What if I could have responded sooner, etc., might R. be alive today? And yet all the wondering will not change the reality that R. is dead and not here, that I will never again in this life feel his touch or hear his voice. I miss my spouse and friend—the man to whom I alone pledged my love publicly. He does dance in spaces no one will ever touch in that way. I discovered things with and about R. and myself that are within me as treasures for the rest of my days!

April 10, 1990

Today would have been R.'s forty-second birthday.

June 17, 1990

I think of R. today because of what he is missing in L.'s life. The tears flow freely. They are tears more of loving than mourning, of fullness than emptiness.

September 2, 1990

Today would have been R.'s and my twelfth wedding anniversary—the fourth one since R. died. I recall memories of our wedding day and the deep joy I knew in committing myself to be with him.

September 4, 1990

The grief I know never ends; it only deepens and fills an ever deeper, quieter space—accessible only by me and to me in solitude. This fall, I sense, I will grieve in a way I have never grieved—for me, for what will never be with R., for my own R. parts. And perhaps as I let go anew, go down into the silent spaces, feel my limits and fatigue, I will only "fall apart" all the more, so that from the ashes, the phoenix can rise anew, determined by a new spirit enlivened within me.

September 27, 1990

Today a colleague's husband is killed suddenly in an accident. It is a Thursday; he is the age R. was when he died. Another broken heart . . .

October 1, 1990

Today is the funeral. R. flashes into my consciousness all day as I picture detailed memories of our life together. I weep from such a deep place, knowing I was in there for the long run and we only had the short run of eight and a half years.

Even after all that I have felt, all the difficult inner work I have done and the healing that has occurred, there is a tiny, raw, wounded, unhealed spot that gets torn open anew by such events as a husband's death and a new widow's pain. And the rising feelings of hope and strength seem dashed against stone in a few brief moments.

October 16, 1990

I dream:

> *L. and I are in a different, smaller home space. R. appears and returns. He is thinner and clean shaven. There is an ambivalence on both our parts about embracing. Finally I take the initiative and hold my arms out in a welcoming and forgiving gesture. There is a sense that nothing could be the same again (which, of course, is true). And then there is a fading of the dream even as I try to grasp its meaning or hold on a little longer.*

October 21, 1990

I thought of R. with such gratitude for buying our home together. A large part of him desired to live such an ordinary life. I was soaring off, probably to offer balance. Now as my desire and willingness to live an ordinary life intensifies, R. is not here to share this.

I miss you in ever new ways, R., feeling robbed. I hope you are at peace and know a depth of contentment. You hold the unique position of being my spouse, and I picture myself being buried beside you when my life comes to an end.

November 3, 1990

I am slowly grasping that the silent shouldering of sorrow asks as much courage as the taking of action.

December 7, 1990

As the snow raged to blizzard proportions, I watched an old musical *The King and I*. I had forgotten that in the story Anna is a widow. I connected with her character in a new way, especially when she sang of her deceased husband, "I've had a love of my own."

Yes! I have had! And that has made all the difference! I was espoused to R. I loved him in a way that I never loved anyone, working on myself to enhance our relationship. I learned to express desire without expectation but with acceptance of the present moment. I was willing to struggle and to hang in there. I loved R. I still do love him.

We made changes in our individual lives and came together to make a home and build a family. I have done that with no other.

As time moves on and I know a healing, I seem to touch an ever deeper grief. Initially after R.'s death, I had to adjust to more generic changes—of not being married, not being a couple, not sharing parenting. And in that light I adjusted routines, patterns, ways of thinking and organizing. As that all falls into a pattern, and I've gone to the depth of feeling in those regards, I am freed to grieve and miss R. for who he was and still is to me.

In my grieving I have worked to let go; perhaps now, I have new space to hold and own R. as still my love. No one can take this from me—I've had a love of my own!—and that does make all the difference. As I allow myself the depth of feeling, perhaps I will know the courage to walk forward on my path.

January 5, 1991

I have friends I can count on emotionally but not practically and not for stability. Stability connotes long-term relating with a degree of commitment and a priority of effort and energy.

February 6, 1991

Today I play and replay a song, "Walk in the World For Me." I remember how poignantly this touched me shortly after R.'s death, as something he could have written and sung to me after his dying. Hearing it today, I know that I have grieved and said good-bye to R.; I also know that he is a part of me and I of him forever! What hit me in a new way is how I have made space in the letting go. What I owned for the first time at this level of depth is that I not only miss being married, but also can hold the idea of remarrying. I miss making a home with someone and sharing dailynesses. I miss being invested with a partner for the future. As I let myself feel this in new ways, the feeling is not based on a desire or wish to remake what was, but rather an acceptance, acknowledgment, and letting go of what was, as well as an acceptance, acknowledgment, and opening up to what could be.

February 8, 1991

Today at work in consulting, a woman recognized my name and related that R. had been a therapist for herself and her husband and really helped them. I was warmed, and when I hung up, I burst into tears, sobbing alone in my office. I toyed with calling someone or even sharing with one of my colleagues and yet had no energy for initiative or explanations.

No one at work has any idea of what I hold or carry. Other's situations are more talkable. The inside kind of mourning I continue isn't. People tire of listening and go their own ways . . . I ache so . . .

February 23, 1991

Today I saw the film *Dances With Wolves* and wept several times. John Dunbar reflects on how he feels as a groom, having eyes only for his beloved, Stands with a Fist. I recalled the soul-magic moments of my own wedding night, taking in R. physically, psychically, emotionally, spiritually—bonding forever. And I wept. This is not an aspect of friendship. I miss having one as the purpose of my devotedness.

February 25, 1991

Today, I choose to pursue a sabbatical leave. I choose something for myself, of which R. will not be a part.

February 26, 1991

Today, I recall the experience of walking with R. on parallel paths, holding hands across the middle untrodden part of the path. The image of that experience was to mark our journey together: pledging our commitment on the one hand, while recognizing that at times one or the other might walk on ahead. And then later, learning to adjust our individual pace to the other's.

And then I recalled the image of the yellow light and R. walking into it alone as he died; I still had to stay and journey.

I let go of my fears of the unknown by staying in the present moment, celebrating with gratitude my choosing!

March 12, 1991—fourth anniversary of R.'s death

Your presence is so keen today, Raymond; but I don't find myself missing you as I did. I have become accustomed to spaces without your touch or look or voice; I have become accustomed to making decisions without you. I have become accustomed to missing you; yet you are in me and with me forever. I wonder how you are and yet have a deep knowing sense that you too have known healing. Each of us is free, in new ways, to love the other. I love you now in the present as I live and care for L., as I honor myself and connect with my inner R. parts, as I choose with more boldness and courage and daring.

This year I do not replay events surrounding your death. Some memories come, but I feel no need or desire to review what is past. I miss missing you, R. I miss missing loving you. You are forever a part of me, integrated into my emerging wholeness even as we are ever more separate. I've had a love of my own, and that has made all the difference. I am grateful for your pledge, your love, your struggle, our life and growth together. L. misses you more and more deeply, unable to directly remember you. Bathe and shower her with the energy of your protective presence, R. In whatever way that is possible to you, I really believe that you have not forsaken us, that you love us, and in that choice suffer much because of the separation, yet know healing and a type of purification.

What a grand reunion you, L., and I will have one day! As I write I connect with a desire to want to re-wear my wedding ring. Whether I do or do not, that desire expresses the connection we have, R. This is inexpressible even to myself, but I know it!

April 12, 1991

Today, at our monthly counselors' meeting, a colleague mentions you, R. A feeling of pride, as well as deep sorrow and sadness, filled me. You were wise and knowledgeable beyond your years in so many arenas, R. You made a difference. I miss you and the energy we shared. We are not finished with each other yet. You dance in my heart forever, dear one. I have a desire to write of you, us, our life together, our life apart. As I root here in this community, I imagine myself, years from now, being buried next to you. I love you with an abiding love, R., spouse and husband, friend and beloved.

Closing

Giving Voice to Remembering

Each year around March twelfth, I receive a note from my sister Jane. Sometimes it just says, "Remembering and thinking of you with love." Other years it may be signed, "I know, I care, I love you, sister."

And each year just before January sixteenth, I write my sister a short similar note. Whatever format these take, they create a bond between us in our remembering.

When we lose someone close to us, time eventually passes and life goes on, but a sorrow still lingers inside of us. Despite the changes and rhythms fostering integration, we carry some element of grief as a continuing legacy. Our task is not to be free of the pain but to live with the suffering, knowing that we are forever changed.

We heal by paying attention to our inner processes. We find some relief in naming our feelings. We release our sorrow when we give voice to our grief. Then we can reconnect with hope and act with courage.

A tree, changing through the seasons, remains connected to its roots, which nourish and sustain its growth. I choose to share these seasons of grieving with the recognition that my growth into deepened understanding continues even as I end the flow of words.

Some of our deepest emotions belong only to ourselves and will never be channeled into words. Other words, spoken at moments of great feeling, we only come to understand and appreciate with time.

I reread our wedding vows, missing R. in ever deeper ways.

R.: . . . And most of all, Margaret, I promise to love you. . . until life passes from me and I enter the final stage of my becoming whole.

M.: . . . Most of all, dear Raymond, I promise to love you tenderly all the days of my life.

I have come to understand that R. has lived out his promise to and through his death. He is gone out there, but he is not gone inside me. He dances in my heart. Knowing a joy no one can take from me, I have had a love of my own.

I continue to live out my promise, for
    LOVE
        does
            not
                come
                    to
                        an
                            end.

Epilogue

We continue to witness the dramatic replay of death in our culture. The media connects us to the famous and not-so-famous around the world who lose a loved one. We make promises to ourselves about living more sensitive, meaningful lives. Yet all too soon, the hype dissipates and we return to our routines and resume familiar patterns.

What occurs when death becomes personal? There is nothing we can do to entirely fill the void left by the death of the one we love. In remembering his impact on our lives, we embrace the emptiness that his absence creates. Mortality is no longer an abstraction happening to people out there.

Remembering is so key to knowing ourselves in the present. For as we remember we integrate the loss, grief, pain and hope into a new way of being. And this silent shouldering of sorrow asks as much courage as the bold taking of action.

Over the years since Raymond's death, I have remained devoted to his memory, helping him "live" and die for our daughter, Laura Hope. I have witnessed the pain of Laura's emptiness again and again as she grows into a young woman, cheated of knowing her father.

Laura was robbed of her innocence at the age of six. Her father delighted in her as only a father can. And yet he has been absent at dance, piano, and voice recitals, birthdays, holidays, on Father's Day, at her high school graduation.

Over the years Laura has written several papers that express her ache. When applying to the Interlochen Arts Academy, she was asked to submit an essay about the person of her choice with whom she had been given the opportunity to spend one day. Laura wrote:

It is not a famous person with whom I would choose to spend a day. It is not someone of whom many people have heard. It is not someone who has impacted the entire world or made some fantastic discovery. It is someone far greater than one who may have accomplished all these things. This is a person who is a true hero to me. He is someone who urges me on, keeping me on a quest to succeed, though only with his spirit. This heroic, supportive, encouraging soul is my father. . . . As I have grown older my understanding has grown also, providing me with very difficult emotions to handle. Though that understanding has grown I am yet to understand.

While at Interlochen, Laura wrote a major fifty-page paper for her "Destiny in Literature" class. This was to be a biography extending through at least seventy years to her death and told through another's eyes. Laura wrote "A Lullaby" using her father's "voice." Through Laura's pen, her Daddy Raymond tells her life story. "She was only a six-year-old child when I left her. If only she knew that though my body could toil no longer, my heart has always been hers." Laura gave voice to words she longed to hear from her father. "A Lullaby" was Laura's amazing expression of the ongoing process of mourning that she has courageously undertaken.

Laura Hope is now a college student studying literature and music. She hopes to teach and perform, marry and have a family. Laura is tall like her father and inherited many of his gifts, which she is developing. However, she is truly her own person. Laura has felt emotions beyond her years, struggling to make sense of her father's early death. Her grief has deepened her empathy and fostered an acute sensitivity to people. Laura's story of growing into a caring and compassionate woman, without her father, is for another book—one that I hope she or we will someday write.

My life has been far different than I had hoped or planned when Raymond and I married in 1978. Raymond's death was a devastating and disorientating experience from which I only wanted relief and escape. And yet, as I have lived widowhood these last thirteen years, I have known healing of my broken heart and crushed spirit. I have been miraculously invited and supported to acknowledge my grief, suffer the pain, and come to know new life through Raymond's death. What has been possible because of my grief? What have I learned?

In missing Raymond's presence as my partner, I have struggled and come to know the strength of my own spirit. While grieving the loss of daily companionship, I have had to:

—re-form my sense of identity
—redefine my sense of family
—restructure ways of parenting alone
—reshape dreams and goals without Raymond

Although widowhood has made me single again, it is not at all the same as my earlier years were. Although alone anew, I have had a love of my own and have known the joys and sorrows of commitment to another. Together we made decisions, solved problems, laughed, and made history. Those experiences all contributed to who I now am alone.

I had looked forward to raising our daughter together and then redefining our life as Laura spread her wings toward independence. Instead, I have ached to share the joys and sorrows of parenting. I made parenting a priority, temporarily suspending career and personal pursuits. Not only did Laura need to be able to count on me, but also we needed to forge new patterns and rituals without Raymond. We have continued to live in the same home with easy access to the cemetery where Raymond is buried. And yet, we have also had the courage to live away for a year in a place where no one knew of Raymond. This experience strengthened each of us to go forward in new and creative ways. When Laura and I returned to our home, we "moved in" as a family of two.

I have learned the value of inner work and its impact on my effectiveness in the outer world. I more readily express my feelings to people today, knowing there may not be a tomorrow. I have grown in empathy toward people who experience loss at any age.

Writing my own story has been therapeutic and strengthening for me. As I become a more mindful listener, I encourage others to tell their story. My words cannot fill the ache, but being with them and listening to their story can be a gift beyond words.

All of this has impacted my work as a professional counselor. I am humbled to accompany others in their journeys toward healing and wholeness. I am grateful when I can foster relationships that encourage people to discover their self-strength. I have worked in schools, private practice, and as a consultant. And now I find myself led to walk with people in the last stages of their journey toward death. I know the strength of my own spirit and am not afraid. Everything has prepared me for this.

As I completed this section, I had a dream:

> I'm embracing Raymond, so thrilled to see him again. He has been given a second chance. We sway and dance a bit. I tell him that I feel freer and better able to tune in to rhythm and movement. I want to dance with him. He holds me close, smiling, saying "my Meig." Then I sense he will be gone again. I don't want to open my eyes. I want to stay in the embrace.

Reluctantly, I open my eyes to the daylight. I want the feelings of the dream to continue. I miss Raymond dearly and long for the comfort of his familiar embrace. I loved him beyond just the practical levels of daily living, and so he is still a part of me. I am open to new love and joy each day because I remember a love.

November 1999
Sandusky, Michigan

Works Cited

Moore, Robert and Gillette, Douglas. 1990. *King, Warrior, Magician, Lover.* San Francisco: Harper; 125.

Potok, Chaim. 1972. *My Name is Asher Lev.* New York: Ballantine; 156.

Rilke, Rainer Maria. 1982. "Lament" in: *The Selected Poetry of Rainer Maria Rilke.* Edited and translated by Stephen Mitchell. New York: Random House; 137.

Rilke, Rainer Maria. 1934/1962/1954. *Letters to a Young Poet.* New York: W. W. Norton & Co., Inc.; 64.

Shuchter, Stephen R. 1986. *Dimensions of Grief (Adjusting to the Death of a Spouse).* San Francisco: Jossey-Bass.

About the Author

Margaret Palczynski Dunbar has a part-time counseling practice in Sandusky, Michigan. Trained as an educator and Licensed Professional Counselor (LPC), she also works as a consultant for the Sanilac Intermediate School District. Margaret cherishes family and friendship, values solitude, and finds solace in nature.